0796930

Learning Skills For The Science Student

Stefan Bosworth, MA
Director, Learning Skills & Tutorial Program,
CUNY Medical School

Marion A. Brisk, Ph.D.
Program Director of Chemistry
CUNY Medical School

H&H Publishing Company, Inc.

H&H Publishing Company Inc.

Copyright 1986 by **H&H** Publishing Company Inc.
2165 Sunnydale Blvd. Suite N
Clearwater, Florida, 33575
Ph (813) 442-7760

Cover Art: Tom Howland
Editor: Katherine Savige
Production: Margaret Burns

ISBN 0-943202-21-3

Printing number is the last number

10 9 8 7 6 5 4 3 2

Acknowledgement

We would like to thank Dr. J. W. Carmichael for developing innovative educational programs at Xavier University, Louisiana, which enabled many students to experience a successful college career and also inspired us to write this book.

Contents

Introduction

In our complex, technological world, learning science is becoming essential for the well-being of both the individual and the society. Science majors who plan careers in industrial science, education, or medicine are entering a competitive area. In order for most people to achieve their potential in the sciences, they need to use special study skills. Students who take the time to develop these skills will maximize their success in science courses and, later, in chosen professions.

This handbook presents a logical, systematic approach to reading textbooks, taking lecture notes, preparing for exams, and taking tests. Common sense procedures explain how to design a study space and manage time. The advantages of study groups are discussed also. These learning skills apply to both elementary and sophisticated techniques of studying science. Thus *Learning Skills for the Science Student* should help science students who want to better their performance, regardless of their educational level.

This book began as a learning skills syllabus for an integrated premedical-medical program. It was expanded to include the medical sciences and, later, all of the sciences. This growth resulted from practical experience with students in all of these disciplines and the observation of recurring problems. Students who adopted the methods described here improved their ability to understand scientific material and increased their exam scores. We are not advocating strict adherence to the methods we present, but instead, suggest that you adapt them to fit your individual style of learning.

The scientific method which gave rise to great discoveries is simply a systematic, logical approach to studying nature. When studying science, you need to develop a similar approach. The skills you develop as a science student will lead to clear logical thinking, which is necessary for success in any endeavor.

One
Designing a Study Space

To be a successful student, one of the most important, yet most often over-looked, steps you can take is to set up an adequate study space. Most students do not think about where they study and simply pick a spot to sit down and start studying. This will lead to inefficiency in studying, lost time, and poor results. A study space can be a whole room or part of a room. It is very important that there be only one study space where all non-library studying can be done.

Your desk, the focus of most of your studying, should enable you to write comfortably and should have some drawers to store study materials: rulers, pencils, pens, and paper. Keep these materials nearby, so you won't have to interrupt your studying to find them. Along with your desk, you need an adequate chair. The chair you choose should not be too comfortable, or you may fall asleep while studying. A folding metal or wooden chair is a good choice.

On top of your desk, you need a lamp which illuminates both sufficiently and evenly. When you are reading the extensive material assigned in science courses, you need lighting which reduces eye fatigue as well as general fatigue. The brightest light is not necessarily the best light. Good lighting means even illumination. Your overhead lighting should also illuminate evenly. Good desk and overhead lighting will make your long study hours easier.

It is a good idea to have a file. In the file you can keep notes from past courses that you think will help you in the future, past exams which can help you study for future exams, research papers (always make a copy of any research paper that you do for a course), and important articles which you have read. All material put in the file should be put in folders and labeled so you can find it later.

You also need a bookcase in your study area. This bookcase should contain all present textbooks so they are easy to find, textbooks from past courses (remember that it is always a mistake to sell textbooks from science courses that you have completed, as they are likely to make good reference material later on), reference books such as medical dictionaries, and practice review books. Magazines like *Scientific American, Science, The New England Journal of Medicine, The Journal of Environmental Science and Technology*, etc. should also be kept here.

Your bookshelf should also store supplemental textbooks for science and math courses in which you are enrolled. It is always a good idea to have supplemental texts for any science and math course that you take. This is because each text explains ideas and concepts differently, and if you do not understand the first explanation, you may understand the second. A good way to pick a supplemental text is to ask the professor what he or she recommends or to ask students who have done well in the course what other text(s) they used. If you can't afford these texts, borrow them from a library or from other students. It is important that the only material on your bookshelf relates either to your current studies or your future career.

Creating a Comfortable Environment

Design your study space to make it most comfortable for you. If that space is only part of a room, set it off from the rest of the room. It is important that you keep things you like here. If you like posters, then there should be posters in the room. If you like plants, then there should be plants in the room. The important idea is that you design your study area around your personality. It is a good idea to paint your study area, particularly if it is only a part of a room. This will not only define the study area for you, but also for other members of the household.

Choose a color with which you feel happy. There is no one perfect color, although lighter colors are often thought to be more conducive to relaxation and comfort than darker colors. It is also a good idea to choose a study space with a window. The fresh air from the window will help keep you alert and the low level distraction that the window provides will actually improve your studying. Good ventilation and moderate temperature in your study space are extremely important for optimum learning. Poor ventilation and excessive heat will make you drowsy and less alert. If windows are not present, use a fan to move the air. You will be able to study longer and more effectively by keeping temperature low and ventilation high.

Items to Omit From Your Study Space

Nothing should be in your study area that does not improve your studying ability. This means that your clothing, novels that you are reading, phones, and any items that you cannot justify in terms of studying do not belong in your study area.

There should not be a television, radio, or stereo in your study area. All these items will greatly reduce your ability to concentrate and increase the amount of time you will need to complete your studying. Of the three above items, television is the worst. If the television is on, you will tend to watch it for at least part of the time and spend less of your study time really studying.

The second worst item mentioned above is the radio; again, you listen to it and become distracted from your concentration. Your studying will be unproductive. The radio is also a particularly disruptive background noise, because, in most cases, the noise switches constantly from music to an announcer talking.

The stereo, while the least harmful of the above items, will still reduce your studying efficiency and substantially increase the time required to complete assignments. You cannot afford to waste this much time.

In many ways, designing an adequate study space simply requires the use of common sense. Basically, the space should be set up to maximize efficiency. Items that will reduce the benefits of study time should not be present, while those items that will improve efficiency should be.

Try to make your study space comfortable and attractive so that you enjoy being in it. Posters, plants, and other decorative items can help to make the long periods spent here more pleasant.

Two
Reading Scientific Textbooks

When reading a scientific textbook or journal, each paragraph must be scrutinized in order to achieve an in-depth understanding of complex principles. Important details of the material must be extracted and understood. Concepts need to be related to each other in order to form a complete picture of the topic being studied. Formulas, charts, and graphs all require analysis and integration with the written material. In short, to get the most from your textbook, develop effective scientific reading skills. Such skills permit clear systematic understanding of the material. Following is a description of a systematic approach to reading textbooks, which, if adopted, will increase what you learn from a textbook.

How to Begin

Every textbook has its own unique organization and style. By understanding the organization and noting special features of the text, you can increase the text's contribution to your knowledge of the material. Generally, the organization and text features have been designed by the authors to present the material in an understandable fashion. Therefore, the first step in understanding your text is to note the title, credentials of authors, and copywrite date to ascertain the currency of the text.

You will save yourself time and energy if you are aware of the contents and location of the special features of your text. They are there to assist you in mastering the material. Carefully examine the table of contents. Note the general organization of the text as well as the nature of the topics. What does the order of the chapters reveal about the material that will be studied? It is especially important to note the presence of appendices, indices and references. What is contained within the appendices? Are there glossaries, answers to questions or problems, tables, etc? Physical constants and other data are frequently provided in the appendix as well. These values will be needed for the problems which appear elsewhere in the text, so familiarize yourself with the tables and charts. Knowing all of this information will enable you to maximize the information you derive from your book.

Find out what is included in all the sections of the book, since you will find that you need some of this material as the course develops. For example, some texts review mathematical operations that are used in some exercises. If you are like most of us you may have forgotten these operations and require a review. Authors frequently are aware of your deficiencies and therefore provide these reviews in the appendix or other sections of the book. Save yourself time by locating useful information right from the beginning.

Chapter Organization

Next, determine the general organization of the chapters in the text. Is there an introduction, a summary, a set of questions and/or problems at the end of the chapter? Are there major topics which are then broken down into subcategories? What special features are used to emphasize material? Authors frequently focus your attention on important information by using one or more of the following methods.

> Italicized print
>
> Bold-faced print
>
> Underlining
>
> Comments in the margins
>
> Shading
>
> Learning objectives
>
> Key terms listed
>
> Differently colored print

Look for these techniques and keep them in mind as you study. Make sure you understand the material which the author(s) have highlighted. Check to see if problems or questions in the back of the text are keyed to specific topics in the chapters. If they are, this feature will be useful to you as you work on individual chapters later.

What kind of illustrations (graphs, tables, charts or diagrams) appear in the text? These are important. Does the author summarize information from the text with charts and diagrams? Key information is contained within these features and by ignoring them, you will miss an important message from the author.

Make sure you understand these features thoroughly as you study. Are there sample problems and exercises within the text? These should be emphasized as you study (see Problem Solving chapter). Only by understanding applications of the material to solving problems and answering questions will you achieve the level of understanding generally required in a science course. Once you are familiar with the general organization of the text and the individual chapters, you are ready to use the book to its fullest potential.

Survey Reading

When you open your text to the chapter assigned, survey the chapter first before you begin reading. Follow these steps:

1.   Note the **title** of the chapter. How does it relate to the chapters that precede and follow it?

2.   Read the **introduction** in order to get a handle on central ideas of the chapter. Often the introduction will relate this chapter to what you've already learned so that you can see how concepts build upon each other.

3.   Read the **headings** and **subheadings** of the chapter in order to determine the topics and subtopics of the chapter. Note the relationship between main topics and subtopics and between each main topic.

4.   Look for **graphs, tables, charts**, or **diagrams**. These features are used by the author to explain important material. Make note of their presence and be certain to study them thoroughly when reading the chapter.

5.   In some science textbooks, **summaries** appear at the end of the chapter. It's a good idea to read these before reading the chapter. Summaries will give you an overview of the material, so you will know what to look for and emphasize.

6.   If there are problems or questions, read them briefly. Your objective in reading the chapter is to gain sufficient understanding of the material, so that you can solve the problems and/or answer the questions. By reading them first, you will have a concept of what you need to be able to do. You can study the chapter with these problems and/or questions in mind. Sample problems often use concepts and principles similar to the problems in the back of the chapter. By reading the problems at the end of the chapter first you will be alerted to the kind of information you need to gather from the chapter. If you follow this procedure, you will not have that frustrated feeling students frequently experience when they attempt to answer problems or questions at the end of chapters and see no relationship between what they just read and what they are asked to answer.

Reasons For Survey Reading

We can think of at least six good reasons for survey reading.

1.   If you survey your reading first, you will increase your understanding and retention of the material when you read the chapter.

2.   By surveying, you acquire a grasp of the important ideas and their relationships. With this focus, the chapter will become more meaningful, and you will find that the problems and/or questions at the end of the chapter are answerable.

3.   An effective means to mastering material of any kind is to ask yourself the right questions. This ability is as important to the science student as it is to the Nobel prize winner. If you survey the material first, you can ask yourself meaningful questions as you read the chapter. Self-questioning improves comprehension and retention. By formulating questions and finding answers, you're thinking about the topics in detail. What are they about? How do they relate to each other? Some examples of the kinds of questions you need to ask yourself as you read will be provided in this chapter. Remember, reading science requires active participation as you are learning.

4.   Another advantage to surveying chapters is that you are then able to predict the approximate time you will need to read the chapter. You can make a reasonable judgment by determining the length and complexity of the chapter along with your knowledge of time spent on similar chapters. Effective time management (see "Time Management" chapter) is critical in fulfilling your potential as a science student.

5.   Surveying identifies the topics of the chapter which you must know in order to construct a useful outline.

6.   In those subjects where you must underline, such as Anatomy, and in other courses which require extensive memorization, surveying the chapter allows you to better distinguish what you need to underline and what you don't, making your underlining more effective.

Reading the Textbook

After surveying the textbook, you are prepared to read the chapters. Does this mean all you need at this point is your text? No. You need to be actively involved in what you are reading. You need to be thinking about the material as you go along, asking and answering your own questions. By **underlining the text**, making **marginal notes** or by **outlining the chapter** as you read, you will be actively involved in the learning process. You need to use your pen, not just your text, in order to maximize your understanding of the work. We recommend that for courses like anatomy which require extensive memorization underlining is best. Courses which emphasize concepts, such as chemistry or physics, or courses where material in the text is not of equal value, such as general biology, outlining is more appropriate. The nature of the course will determine the method for you to get the most out of your textbook. Remember that for most science courses, outlining is the preferred method. Courses that require underlining are the exception in science, not the rule.

Techniques for Textbook Marking and Underlining

Guidelines to Underlining

The purpose of underlining is to focus your attention on the essential information. Frequently, in their zeal to master the material, students underline everything, feeling all of the information is critical. In doing so, they defeat the purpose of the activity. Only the essential information should be underlined. The reason for this is really twofold:

1.   If you underline only important information, when you read
       the chapter again later for review, you will be able to focus on
       central ideas;

2.   In order to underline important material, you need to be thinking
       actively about what you are reading, and only by doing this are you
       really learning.

Read the paragraph or paragraphs under a topic before underlining. You can better identify the information if you read the material first and then go back and underline. After you have read the paragraph or section, ask yourself the following questions:

1.   What is the central idea or concept of this section? Frequently, the section heading will be helpful in answering this question.

2.   What other concepts or relationships are contained within this section and how are they connected to the central issue?

Based on your responses to these questions, you will be able to go back and identify information that should be underlined. By following this procedure, you will think about the material, and increase your understanding and retention. Also, you will become aware of whatever is unclear or doesn't make sense to you. In the process of learning, it is just as vital to identify what you don't understand, as well as what you do know.

Use some system to identify what you don't understand and need to work on. You can asterisk the paragraph(s) or use question marks. Even comments inserted in the margins can be used as a system to flag your attention to material that must be clarified.

In Summary

1.   Read the paragraph or section first.
2.   Underline only key information.
3.   Use some consistent method to indicate material that needs clarification.

Carefully examine the underlined material presented below.   Then try underlining the other paragraphs using our suggestions.

Practice Passages
Amos Turk, Jonathan Turk, Janet T. Wittes, Robert E. Wittes, *Environmental Science*.
W. B. Saunders Company, 1978

FOSSIL FUEL DEPOSITS

Coal is a valuable geological deposit that was formed from organic debris such as decayed animal and vegetable matter (fossils). As each layer of this ancient organic debris started to decompose, it was gradually covered by successive layers, and so the decomposition was interrupted before it was complete. Thus some of each layer was preserved under new layers of sediment and debris. The combined heat and pressure from accumulating layers initiated a series of transformations that changed the underground plant tissue into coal.

Go to a swamp or marsh and dig up a shovelful of the muck on the bottom. If you examine it closely, you will find that there may be very little dirt in your sample; it is mostly decayed plant matter. If such a swamp bottom is covered with inorganic sediment and compressed for hundreds of thousands of years, a small coal deposit will develop. However, most modern swamps are poor coal producers. It is estimated that a layer of compressed organic debris 12 meters (39 ft) thick is required to produce a 1-m layer of coal. For a layer this large to accumulate, conditions must be favorable and stable in a region for a great many years. Coal deposits probably are being formed today in many areas, notably in the Ganges River delta in India, but the process is extremely slow - much, much slower than the exploitation of existing reserves. Therefore, since we cannot expect formation of new deposits to keep pace with use, we have all the more reason to conserve our present reserves.

Oil and gas are also organic deposits, but these fuels were probably formed from tiny marine microorganisms rather than from the debris of large plants. As microscopic sea creatures settled to the bottom of the ocean and were later covered with mineral sediment, tiny droplets of body oils were squeezed out of each organism. If the rock formation was favorable, this oil was trapped into large deposits and altered chemically by heat and pressure until petroleum was formed.

MATERIALS AND ENERGY

A natural ecosystem is stable when the various processes that take place in it are in balance. Birth and death, growth and decay, the absorption of nutrients and the elimination of wastes -- all of these processes involve the cycling of materials and the flow of energy. When any one material becomes depleted, as for example when the water supplies are exhausted by pine trees on the eastern slope of the Colorado Rockies (see Section 4.9), the entire system is upset. Similarly, if the flow of energy is disrupted, as when phytoplankton in a body of water are destroyed by an oil spill, the system is again thrown out of balance. Human systems are also delicately dependent on the maintenance of an orderly supply of materials and energy. To survive in a developed society we need food, fuel, clothing, shelter, and networks of transportation. Each of these needs can be supplied only if both energy and materials are widely available. Most of the food consumed by people in industrial nations is grown on commercial farms. The farmers use tractors made of steel, structural material, and powered by gasoline, a fuel. Agricultural fertilizers are usually materials that are mined or chemically manufactured, transported, and spread on the fields with machines powered by fossil fuels.

Materials and energy are intimately interrelated in our modern world. Think of an oil well. Drilling for oil requires specialized material. For example, steel is used for the drilling materials. For example, steel is used for the drilling rig, diamond or carborundum chips for the augers, and copper or aluminum wire for the electrical system. Products made from oil help mine the metals needed to build the equipment to drill for oil. The drilling rig itself needs fuel (which comes from oil) to drive the drill. If any material or fuel is unavailable and no substitutes are found, the entire system will fail. Both the developed and the developing world must ask, "How stable is our cycle of materials, and how reliable is our energy flow, and how long can they be expected to last?"

First, we must understand how energy differs from matter, or material substances. Wood, sand, and iron are materials, and they consist of atoms that retain their identity despite physical or chemical transformations. Thus, one can take a bar of iron, beat it, roll it into a sheet, shred it into pieces, melt it, and allow it to solidify again, and one would still have iron. If the bar of iron is set outside in damp air, it will react chemically with oxygen to produce iron oxide, commonly called rust, but even this chemical conversion does not destroy iron atoms. The iron can be easily recovered from its oxide and reconverted to the pure metal. Moreover, chemical and physical operations can be repeated again and again; the iron atoms never get "tired," or destroyed. At the end of any conceivable set of chemical processes, the original supply of iron atoms remains.

Energy, on the other hand, is not a material. Energy is defined as the capacity to perform work or transfer heat. Where does energy go after it has been used? The carbon atoms in a lump of coal unite with oxygen as the coal burns, and its inorganic content turns to ash, but what becomes of its energy? This nonsubstance, called "the capacity to do work", is elusive and hard to keep track of. If we can find used iron and reuse it, why can't we find used energy and reuse it? Or better yet, if energy isn't really matter could we find some for nothing? These two questions plagued scientists for a long time and the search for answers led to the study of heat-motion, or thermodynamics.

Outlining

It is best, if possible, to outline reading assignments. Outlining forces you to identify central ideas and understand their relationships. Outlines are also very useful as study aids for exam and lecture preparation. Outlining reading assignments before attending lecture will increase your understanding of the lecture. Most professors present material in outline form; several main ideas or concepts are presented along with their relationships. Outlining before class will make the lecture clear and understandable.

How to Outline Effectively

Most science texts are presented in outline form with each major topic clearly indicated and subtopics following (see examples). The student must include information explaining these central and side issues showing their relationships as well. Be sure to provide only enough information to adequately explain the material. If too much unnecessary material is included, the outline will lose its versatility and take on the appearance of the text itself. Be selective and concise.

The method of outlining that is recommended is a skeleton outline. This simply means that, instead of using whole sentences in your outline you will use the shortest possible phrase that expresses the topic that you are outlining.

As mentioned before, outlining is a particularly effective way of using the science textbook, since most science textbooks are written in outline form; main points are highlighted in large print and sub points in print that is larger than the regular print on the page but not as large as the main points. Then you need to fill in enough detail so that you can completely understand the topic. One way of testing whether your outline is complete is to turn each topic and subtopic into a question and see if you can answer that question by reading your notes. You will find in most cases, especially after lectures are presented on the topics outlined or after solving problems or answering questions, that some additional information is required or some alterations are in order. Outlines tend to be modified as your knowledge and comprehension expands, so its a good idea to leave sufficient space for these additions when you are first developing the outline.

Outlining your textbook will be extremely useful at exam time, as these notes will prove to be an effective and concise way of reviewing the material, and in most cases, you will not need to re-read the relevant chapters. These notes will also be very helpful later on when preparing for such exams as the M.C.A.T., the National Boards Part I and II in Medicine, the National Boards in pharmacology and many other generalized exams. In order to use these notes at exam time and later on be sure to file them in a safe place.

Carefully review the example of outlining provided below. Try to complete the outline on your own. A practice reading and outlining exercise is shown on the next four pages.

Practice Passage
Frank Brescia, John Arents, Herbert Meislichand and Amos Turk,
Fundamentals of Chemistry, Academic Press, 1980

12.11 COLLIGATIVE PROPERTIES OF SOLUTIONS

The vapor pressure of each substance in a solution is less than the vapor pressure of the pure substance. For the solvent in a dilute solution, we have a general relationship-Raoult's law- for how much less the vapor pressure is. The remarkable thing about this law is that it says nothing about what the solute is. All that appear are the mole fraction of the solvent and the vapor pressure of the pure solvent. This means that one solute is as good as another for lowering the vapor pressure of a given solvent. As a result of the lowering of vapor pressure, several other things happen to a solvent when something is dissolved in it: Its boiling point is raised, its freezing point is depressed, and its osmotic pressure is increased. At least one of these effects is very familiar: Antifreeze is added to an automobile radiator to keep the water from freezing in winter, that is, to lower its freezing point. These four properties-vapor-pressure depression, boiling-point elevation, freezing-point depression, and osmotic pressure- are known as colligative properties. Their common feature is that they depend on the mole fraction of the solute, not on its identity; that is, these properties depend on the relative number of solute molecules, not on the kind of molecules. We will now study how large these effects are and how they can be used to obtain interesting information.

12.12 VAPOR-PRESSURE DEPRESSION

Raoult's law says that, in any dilute solution, the vapor pressure of the solvent A is approximately equal to the mole fraction of A times the vapor pressure of pure A:

$$P_{solvent} = P^0_{solvent} \ x_{solvent}, \ \text{or} \ P_A = x_A P_A{}^0.$$

Let us assume that there is only one solute, B. Then

$$x_{solvent} = 1 - x_{solute}$$

$$x_A = 1 - x_B$$

and after substitution, Raoult's law may be written

$$P_A = (1 - x_B) \ P_A{}^0$$

$$P_A = P_A{}^0 - x_B P^0{}_A$$

or, by rearrangement,

$$P_A^0 - P_A = x_B P_A^0$$

This equation illustrates how we can use Raoult's law to calculate the small difference between the vapor pressure of a solvent and that of a dilute solution (Section 12.10). The quantity $P_A^0 - P_A$ is the vapor-pressure depression caused by the addition of the solute to the solvent.

12.13 FREEZING-POINT DEPRESSION AND BOILING-POINT ELEVATION

Let us try out two common antifreezes, ethylene glycol ($C_2H_6O_2$) and methanol (CH_3OH). We prepare a series of solutions of each solute in water and measure the freezing point as follows: The more solute we put in, the more the freezing point is depressed below 0°C -- not surprising. However, the same mass percentage does not correspond to the same depression for the two solutes. This is also not surprising; freezing-point depression is supposed to be a colligative property, dependent on the number of moles of solute rather than the number of grams. We might get similar results for the two solutes if we compared solutions with the same mole percent. This is a good idea, but it is customary to express freezing-point depression in terms of another measure of composition, the molality. The molality, m, of a solution is

$$m = \frac{\text{moles of solute}}{\text{kilograms of solvent}}$$

We may also refer to m as the molality of the solute or the molality of the solution with respect to the solute. When there is more than one solute (B, C, ...), we must identify the molality with respect to each (m_B, m_C, ...).

The freezing-point depression is the difference between the freezing points of the pure solvent and of the solution:

$$\Delta t_f = t_f - t'$$

where t_f is the freezing point of the pure solvent and t_f' is the freezing point of the solution. For the 2.00% solution of ethylene glycol,

$$\Delta t_f = 0°C - [-0.60°C] = .60°C$$

For each of our six solutions, we calculate the molality and the ratio of the freezing-point depression to the molality, with the results shown in Table 12.4.

Not only is the ratio approximately constant for each solute, but it is about the same for one solute as for the other. Indeed, the same ratio is obtained for any solute in water. We may therefore write the equation

$$\Delta t_f = \kappa_f m$$

where K_f is a constant characteristic of the solvent, called the freezing-point depression constant, and m is the molality of the solution. For water the best value is K_f = 1.86°C kg/mol. Table 12.5 shows K_f for some common solvents.

A solution boils at a higher temperature than the pure solvent. The boiling-point elevation is

$$\Delta t_b = t_f - t_f'$$

where t_b is the boiling point of the pure solvent and t_b' is the boiling point of the solution. The elevation is also approximately proportional to the molality of the solution:

$$\Delta t_b = \kappa_b m$$

K_b is the boiling-point elevation constant, which is also given in Table 12.5.

Sample Outline

I   **Colligative Properties** - prop. of solvent which changes when a solute is dissolved in it - prop depends on x_{solute} not identity of solute

    A.   Vapor Pressure Depression -
           vapor pressure of solvent decreases with addition of solute
           1 - Apply Raoult's Law:

$$P_{solvent} = x_{solvent} P^o_{solvent} \qquad \text{p of pure solvent}$$

$$\begin{cases} P_A = x_A P_A \\ x = 1 - x_B \\ P_A = (1 - x_B)P^o_A = P^o_A - x_B P^o_A \end{cases} \qquad \begin{aligned} A &= \text{solvent} \\ B &= \text{solute} \end{aligned}$$

$$\text{Vapor Pressure Depression} \qquad P^o_A - P_A = x_B P^o_A$$

B.   Freezing Point Depression $= \Delta t_f = t_f - t_f'$

$t_f =$ freezing pt. of pure solvent $t_f' =$ freezing pt. of solution

1. $$\boxed{\Delta t_f = K_f m}$$

$K_f =$ freezing point of depression constant (depends on solvent)

$m =$ molality of the solution

$K_f (H_2O) = 1.86^\circ C \dfrac{kg}{mole}$

2.   *Example*
      Antifreeze added to a car radiator to lower freezing point of water.

Try to finish the outline on your own.

Writing Marginal Notes

Writing marginal notes is not by itself an effective means of learning from your textbook. However, in combination with underlining or outlining, it can be helpful. Examples of effective use of margin notes include:

a.   To indicate material that is unclear or contradictory. This focuses your attention on the material which needs to be clarified. Specific questions can be inserted in the margin to help you identify the problem.

b.   To emphasize importance of graphs, tables, etc., especially if they are discussed by the lecturer.

c.   Additions to the text to help explain material. Students, as well as professors, find that there are sections of texts which are poorly written and confusing. Although these sections tend to be small in number, students often need to take their own notes on this material so that it makes sense to them. These clarifications or rewording of the material could be inserted in the margin of the text effectively.

Three
Effective Listening and Notetaking

How to Get the Most Out of the Lecture

Effective notetaking is a necessary skill for success in any science course. You take notes in class to develop a comprehensive record of the professor's ideas so they can be thoroughly studied and understood later. Think of your notes as a handwritten book. If your notetaking skills are poor, your book will be incomplete and inaccurate, and your knowledge of the subject will be the same. Your exam scores will reflect your insufficient knowledge. This is the reason for developing effective notetaking skills; so you can produce a handwritten book from which you can study the material successfully.

Students generally develop some sort of notetaking system during their education. This crucial process of sorting out, organizing, and committing to memory appropriate material is mostly subconscious. It is difficult for you to improve these skills on your own when you are unaware of the process. There are, however, steps that you can follow to improve notetaking skills. These steps comprise a scientific approach to notetaking and, all students, regardless of their individual style, can benefit from studying and applying this approach.

The system described on the following pages is simple and efficient and will make the time you spend in lecture more valuable.

Preparing For a Lecture: Have the Right Tools

You will become an effective notetaker only if you use the right tools. These necessary tools include the pens, paper, and notebooks which are especially suitable for science courses. Format is also important; the way you use space on your paper can either aid or hinder notetaking.

Notebook

A large three-ring binder is strongly suggested for science courses. During the course of the semester, a great deal of written material from class and text book notes will be generated. In addition, you want to include all handouts, diagrams, and solved problems in this loose leaf binder. By keeping everything in one notebook, you will know where to find all of your notes, which is especially helpful before an exam.

A loose leaf notebook also permits easy organization; handouts can be inserted in appropriate spots along with solved problems. Quizzes and exams should also be incorporated since they are useful in preparation for final exams. Notes can be arranged in either chronological or topical order and lecture notes can be easily interspersed with textbook notes.

Pens and Format

Use a pen to take notes. Pencils typically fade with time and can also smear. Use a pen that feels comfortable, so you can write clearly and efficiently. Pencils are useful for solving problems, because it often takes several tries before the problem is solved correctly.

Adopting a specific format will make your notetaking efficient. We suggest a page with a small side margin. The main part of the page is used for class notes, and the side column is reserved for additional comments you insert after class. Use this side space to consolidate and embellish the information presented by the professor. Key points should also be highlighted for easy recognition. The space below is, as already mentioned, where your class notes appear.

Diagram of Page

Your Additions and Clarifications	Class Notes Taken

Only one side of the paper should be used for taking notes. The back side of your paper should be used mainly for adding new materials which might be helpful in understanding the information recorded in your notes. This could include graphs, tables, diagrams or handouts.

Before Each Lecture

First come prepared. It is very difficult to take good notes when you start a lecture unprepared, because you have no idea about the content of the lecture. Students who attend lectures unprepared find lecture notetaking almost impossible, because they cannot distinguish the important from the unimportant information. Students who have prepared for lecture have a general idea of what to expect, so their notes reflect the major points presented. Here are some ways to prepare for a lecture.

Read All Assignments That Are Listed Before the Lecture

The required reading will introduce you to the topics covered by the professor in lecture and give you a frame of reference for your notes. If you do this assigned reading prior to the lecture, your notes will be more meaningful.

Understand How the Professor Uses the Lecture

Professors use lectures for different purposes. If you are aware of the purpose of the lecture, you will know what is important about the lecture and what should be included in your notes. Lecturers generally have one or more of the following objectives in mind:

1.   Explain and clarify material from the readings.

2.   Present new information that is not specifically in the readings, but is related to the topic.

Lecturers generally present material in the form of:

a.   definitions and terms

b.   ideas and concepts

c.   applications and examples

d.   factual information

Your method of notetaking will change depending on the kind of presentation. If a series of terms and definitions is presented, you will want to record them separately, but also show their connection. The same is true of ideas and concepts; note the relationship between them. Record specific examples where possible, since examples help clarify material. Some or all of these modes of presentation may be used in any one lecture.

Review Previous Notes on the Lecture Topic Before Coming to Class

Lectures make more sense if you think of how they relate to past lectures and to the assigned readings. You can do this by looking over your lecture and textbook notes the evening before class. Lectures are generally planned so that each one develops from the prior lecture. Concepts generally build on those presented in previous lectures. Usually, the material follows the reading, and textbook notes help prepare for the lecture.

You must prepare for a lecture in order to really understand the professor. Only with adequate preparation will you be able to take complete and accurate notes.

During the Lecture

How do you decide what to write down? Obviously, you can't record all that is said in the lecture, but you want to write down enough so your notes can be used for study. You must be selective. Record information in outline form; write down the main points and supporting information in a logical order. Use the lecturer's words as much as possible. Some instructors make an effort to indicate their main points by saying, "The main idea is. . . ," or, "We can conclude that," or, "It is important to note." Be on the alert for these signals indicating the main ideas which you should record. Also, look for the hand gestures or voice intonation which some professors use to emphasize main points. Write your notes clearly and concisely so they make sense in the weeks and months ahead.

Title each lecture and all the main topics. Use a skeleton outline when taking notes. This will highlight main points and emphasize the relationship between main points and subpoints as well as between different main points. Using an outline format imposes a structure on your notes. When you organize the lecture material in outline form, concepts and their relationships stand out. Notes in this form are extremely useful for exams; main headings can help construct sample test questions.

Examples are very important in understanding scientific material; highlight them in your notes. Examples or sample problems increase your understanding of the work because they clarify and explain complex concepts and ideas. Try to find some additional examples of your own. These could come from the course text or other relevant textbooks. Old exams might also contain similar examples of the principles being discussed.

Make sure you copy down all the information. Ask yourself how the lectures relate to the textbook. If you know what role the lecture has in the course, you can understand the overall themes of the course better.

If the instructor summarizes, listen closely. Take notes carefully during this summary, since the professor is helping you organize your notes and emphasizing what is important. Summaries cover the information that the professor feels is most important and will use in exams. It will benefit you to take particularly good notes on the professor's summation.

During lecture, professors answer questions raised by students. Usually, these questions involve material which was not clear in the lecture. The professor's explanation provides the student with a more detailed description of the points which were vague. By recording both the questions of other students and the answers of the professor, you will have more information to help you understand the topic. If you have further questions on the material, be sure to ask the professor after class or during office hours. Never let a question go unanswered, for it may be critical in understanding the material and seriously affect your performance on exams.

How to Record Information

You cannot possibly write as rapidly as a lecturer can speak, so you need to learn to record only key words. Only by doing this will you be able to keep up with the lecturer. Make an effort to record as few words as possible and still include the main ideas of the lecture.

Below are some specific suggestions which will help you to record information accurately and sufficiently.

1. Avoid using complete sentences. Record key words which will convey the ideas. For example; if the professor says "coefficients in a balanced chemical equation are used to convey molar ratios," you should write:

    coefficients -balanced equation $\rightarrow$ molar ratios.

2. Don't attempt to use your own words, because it is too time consuming. You can do this later when reviewing and consolidating your notes.

3. Use abbreviated forms of words only if those forms are fairly standard. Use N_2 for nitrogen, cm for centimeter, eq for equation, etc. Use the same abbreviation consistently. Be careful not to abbreviate words which you will not recall after the lecture. Stick to abbreviations that are widely used.

4. There are well-known symbols that you should use frequently, such as arrows indicating a relationship between ideas, equal signs, etc. In addition, some symbols are particularly useful for courses in which mathematical relationships are involved. Some of these are listed in the following table on the next page. Consistent use of symbols will enable you to record some information more accurately.

Frequently Used Mathematical Symbols

Symbol	Meaning
$\propto$	proportional to
$\uparrow$	increasing
$\downarrow$	decreasing

$\neq$	not equal to
$>$	greater than
$<$	less than
$\approx$	approximately
$\equiv$	equivalent to
Δ	difference between two quantities
Σ	sum

5.   As already indicated, use a skeleton outline when taking lecture notes so that main points are highlighted and relations between points can be see.

Examples of Efficient Notetaking

Boyle's law states that pressure and volume are inversely related at constant temperature.

Notes

        Boyle's law $\frac{1}{v}$ p $\propto$ $\Delta T = 0$

According to Charles' law, volume is directly related to temperature under conditions of constant temperature.

Notes

        Charles' law   V $\propto$ T $\Delta P = 0$

An abscess is simply an excessive accumulation of pus in a confined space.

Notes

        abscess = accumulation - pus - confined space

These suggestions enable you to take complete and accurate notes in very little time. The best way to develop these skills is through practice. Use the passages below to practice notetaking. In taking notes on the paragraphs below, use your system of abbreviations and symbols, eliminate unessential information, and use an outline format.

Practice Passages
This passage is taken from:
Frank Brescia, John Arents, Herbert Meislich, and Amos Turk,
Fundamentals of Chemistry. Academic Press. 1980

RADIOACTIVITY

Radioactivity is associated with unstable nuclei. But it is not easy to predict whether a given isotope is radioactive or how it transforms (decays). We have already seen that a greater nuclear stability is associated with a magic number of nucleons. Thus, although $^{208}_{82}$ PB is stable, $^{210}_{82}$ PB is radioactive. The influence of one neutron in stabilizing the nucleus of $^{3}_{2}$ He prompts us to look for a general relationship between nuclear stability and the neutron/proton ratio of nuclei.

In the light elements the ratio $\frac{N \text{ (number of neutrons)}}{Z \text{ (number of protons)}}$ is close to 1. However, in the heavier stable elements the ratio of neutrons to protons increases to about 1.5. Apparently, relatively more neutrons are needed in the heavier nuclei to dilute the electrostatic repulsion between the protons. If some of these neutrons were replaced with protons, the electrostatic repulsion between them would make the nucleus unstable. All nuclei with atomic numbers greater than 83 are radioactive. Of these, only $^{235}_{92}$ U, $^{238}_{92}$ U, and $^{232}_{90}$ Th occur on the Earth in relatively large amounts. The only stable nuclei that contain fewer neutrons than protons are $^{1}_{1}$ H and $^{3}_{2}$ He. It is of interest to note that about 86% of the nuclei in the Earth's crust (excluding water) have even mass numbers.

Nuclei outside the stability band spontaneously transform (decay) to nuclei closer to or within the stability band. Nuclei to the right of the stability band have a relative excess of protons and transform by emission of $^{0}_{+1}$B, $^{1}_{1}$ H, or $^{4}_{2}$ He, or by electron capture. The reaction decreases the number of protons, while the number of neutrons in a reactant nucleus may be unchanged, increased, or decreased depending on the reaction.

PROTEINS

Proteins are condensation polymers of amino acids and have molecular weights in the range of 6000 to 50,000. A protein may be characterized according to its primary and secondary structures. The primary structure of a protein shows the sequence of linkages of amino acid monomers in the protein molecule, without regard to conformation or hydrogen bonding. The first formulation of this kind was reported in 1955 by Frederick Sanger for the protein insulin. The secondary structure of a protein is determined by the spatial arrangement of the polypeptide chain. Evidence obtained mainly from x-ray diffraction patterns has shown that the chain is typically wound into a helix. The helical form is maintained by hydrogen bonds located at spaced intervals.

The entire structure is called alpha-helix. Other secondary structures of proteins include pleated sheets and random coils. Proteins that catalyze biochemical reactions are called enzymes. They are very highly specific, each enzyme being capable of catalyzing only a particular reaction of one type of substance. A cell therefore contains hundreds of enzymes, nearly as many as there are biochemical reactions in the cell. This high specificity implies that spatial effects, in addition to interactions of functional groups, are critical in enzyme action, because there are many more possible shapes of molecules than there are different types of chemical bonds. Figure 23.8 shows a model of an enzyme-catalyzed decomposition of a molecule. Under the influence of the approaching molecule, the enzyme bends so as to grip the molecule in a perfect fit. A complex is formed in which chemical bonds within the molecule are weakened so that decomposition occurs more rapidly than it would without the enzyme.

Use of Notes: Consolidation and Development

We have already discussed two phases of effective notetaking namely preparation for the lecture and the actual notetaking during the lecture. There is a third phase which is as crucial as the other two. This post lecture phase consists of properly preparing your notes for future use. Keep in mind that you want to study from your notes weeks, months, or even years after they are recorded. The only way that notes taken today can be meaningful tomorrow is through appropriate editing.

Lecture notes should be organized systematically. This takes place after the notes have been recorded and is as necessary to effective notetaking as preparation for the lecture and the actual notetaking itself. In order to use your notes most effectively in studying for a course, this post lecture phase is crucial.

Since we tend to forget material almost immediately after the lecture, it is best to edit, organize, and add to your notes at the earliest possible time. The longer you wait, the less able you will be to efficiently consolidate your notes, since you will remember less and less as time goes on.

The first step involves reading through your notes, rewriting words which are not legible, writing out words which you abbreviated and might not remember weeks later, correcting spelling errors, and filling in blank spaces. Any diagrams or visual aids used in lecture which are unclear in your notes should be redrawn so they are accurate. Use your text, other references, or the instructor to provide you with sufficient information to clarify these visualizations. As you read through your notes, make sure that you look up whatever you don't understand. Ask your professor or classmates about material that is unclear. **Never** forget to research those areas that you are uncertain about. Get answers to your questions as soon as possible, and add information to your notes. If there is not a logical flow to your notes, reorganize them so that the main points of the lecture are clear. Remember, your knowledge of the lecture will fade rapidly, so your notes must be read and amended at the first opportunity after the lecture.

With classroom notes, it is a good idea at the end of each day to type or rewrite your notes once you have finished editing them. This is useful because classroom notes tend to be sloppy. Clear and well-organized notes will be very useful to you later when you are studying for an exam or referring to past lectures. In addition, rewriting or typing enhances your retention of material. When you meet with your study group bring your lecture notes for the week. Use part of your study group time to read over the lecture notes of other study group members. This is an excellent way to both better understand the material and make sure you did not miss any important material in lecture.

This post lecture phase to good notetaking not only produces meaningful, useful notes, but also adds to your understanding of the material. In order to improve your notes, you have to think about the material: question what you do and do not understand.

You are actually studying the material during this phase of notetaking and increasing your chances of success in the course. If you keep up with the work in this manner, the course becomes less difficult and more gratifying. Your interest will increase in the material as it becomes less confusing. The more you understand the more you will want to understand, as you witness your own success.

How to Take Useful Lecture Notes (Summary)

1. *Prepare for the lecture.*
   Read all assignments. Know how the professor
   is using the lecture. Review previous lectures on
   the topic as well as relevant textbook notes.
   Bring the needed materials, pens and notebook,
   for lecture notetaking.

2. *During the lecture listen actively.*
   Think about what you're writing down whenever
   possible. Ask questions about points that are
   unclear. If you have adequately prepared, your
   questions will be good ones. By raising
   questions, you are participating in the course,
   and learning becomes more enjoyable for
   instructor and student alike. In addition, by
   actively participating, you are thinking about the
   material and your knowledge expands.

3. *Develop and apply a consistent method of notetaking.*
   Include abbreviations and symbols, and indicate
   relationships between points made by the lecturer.

4. *Record notes in outline form and store them in a large
   three ring binder.*
   This permits you to easily move your notes
   around when organizing and editing them.

5. *Leave spaces when you take notes, especially if you're
   confused about a particular point.*
   After the lecture you can add to your notes so that
   points are explained more clearly.

6. *Don't try to take down everything said by the lecturer.*
   Listen for the main points and record the
   instructor's words as often as possible.

7. *Listen for cues used by your instructor to alert you to
   important points.*
   Your instructor will normally indicate transitions
   from one point to the next and repeat material for
   emphasis. Take special note of material that is
   written on the board, on overhead transparencies,
   or presented on slides.

8. *Lecturers frequently attempt to present a few primary points and several less important points within a lecture period.*
Look for the points without getting lost in the examples provided or explanatory material. Don't lose sight of what is really being emphasized. If you lose track, ask yourself what major point this supplementary material enhances. Reading the assignments before class will be particularly helpful.

9. *Don't be concerned about the neatness of your notes during the lecture.*
Make sure you can read the notes that day so they can then be reworked and made clear for your use in the future.

10. *Record everything written on the blackboard or on an overhead projection.*
Professors generally only write information that they feel is important and likely to appear on exams. Integrate what your professor writes with the rest of the lecture. This is particularly important; otherwise, this material will be confusing when you study it later.

11. *Sit near the front of the lecture hall or classroom.*
There are fewer distractions and you can see and hear better. Also, your attention to the lecture is less likely to fade and your time in class will be well spent. Your questions are also more likely to be answered when you sit at the front of the class. You will get to class on time and tend to be better prepared, since you are in full view of the instructor.

12. *Record assignments and suggestions accurately.*
Ask questions if you are not clear on what needs to be done.

13. *After class review your notes as soon as possible.*
Be sure, while reviewing your lecture notes, to edit and reorganize them.

14. *Rewrite or type your classroom notes after each class.*
This will make the notes more useful later.

15. *Compare your notes to those of your study group.*
Make sure your notes are accurate and complete.

Four
Taking and Preparing for Exams

In medical, pre-medical, and science programs, the primary measure of your understanding of the material presented during the course of the semester is your performance on exams. Your ability to prepare for exams is going to be crucial in determining your success as a student. The key word to preparing effectively for an exam is **organization.** You need to put your lecture, textbook notes, handouts, and problems into a coherent form so you can review all of the material. As you study from week to week, you're dealing with individual concepts and facts; when you review, however, you must integrate all of this material. How are these concepts related? How are they different? In order to remember facts you need to see their relationship. Sort and classify these facts, and you should remember them. Reviewing effectively is a systematic procedure.

Effective review also determines what material is important for the exam so you can condense your studying. We present procedures and suggestions here which, if followed, will improve your test scores.

Exams generally fall into two main categories; essay and objective . Objective exams generally consist of a short answer format while essay types require a discussion or application of concepts and ideas. Each calls for different techniques of studying; however, there are some general approaches to exam preparation that should be used for every exam.

When preparing for a major exam, one should start well in advance of the exam date. Students often wait until the last minute to study for a major exam. This allows anxiety to build up and make your studying less productive. As a consequence, exam performance is far lower than your potential. Since a schedule of major exams is usually given out at the beginning of each semester, a major exam should not come as a surprise to you. It is a good idea to start your preparation for a major exam at least four weeks before that exam is to be given. Find out the format and content of the exam from your instructor before you begin studying. If it is a final exam for example, it may or may not emphasize the work from the last exam. Your exam preparation should reflect this emphasis. If it is mostly problem-solving, spend most of your review time solving problems. Will it be objective, essay, or a combination of both? Open or closed book? Try to obtain exams from previous years. Former students, or sometimes professors, can provide them. As you study for the upcoming exam, make sure you know the material which was tested. Answer the questions and solve problems appearing on these old exams for practice. Some instructors frequently test the same material, since they feel it is particularly important. Be aware, however, that some instructors do not follow clear patterns, so it is best to use your text, lecture notes, and handouts as guides to what is important along with previous exams. If you have been following the other study suggestions in this book, to some extent you have been preparing for the exam all along; however, it is important to do some additional preparation to be successful taking a major science exam.

How to Prepare For an Exam

At least four weeks before a major exam you should add two to four hours a week into your study schedule specifically for preparation. The amount of time you need for preparation depends on the amount and complexity of the material which will be tested. If the exam is the final for a year long course, then most likely you will require more than four weeks for adequate preparation. If the material is particularly complex, adequate exam preparation will demand more than four weeks and additional hours per week. This time should be used for reviewing material which is covered by the exam. Because of the massive amounts of material science students are generally required to master, a system for review is imperative. You must learn to organize and integrate all of the concepts and details in order to understand and remember them. Learning ideas separately limits both understanding and retention of the overall subject, and lowers exam peformance. How do you gather what initially appears to be separate concepts and information into some coherent form and understand and remember it all? The nature of this material largely determines your method of organization.

Category I

Review of Topics Involving Many Concepts and Ideas

If the work encompassed by the exam is largely of a conceptual nature involving numerous relationships, formulas, and their applications, you should construct a general outline as you review for the exam. Optimally, you will already have developed outlines on individual textbook chapters so that information from these outlines can be used for your general outline as well. The benefits of constructing this general outline are the following;

1.   You will become aware of the connection between concepts and ideas discussed in different chapters and lectures. Their similarities, differences, and individual applications will become more apparent. Because exam questions are not organized around single concepts, you must bring together the relevant concepts in answering the questions. By constructing this general outline, you will be integrating the material to gain a thorough understanding of the work.

2.   By developing the outline, you are at the same time studying the material. Therefore, your understanding and overall knowledge is expanding.

3.   These outlines should be saved for final exams and subsequent courses. You will find that many concepts learned in one course are used and elaborated upon in others. You may need to review what was learned in prior courses, and your outlines provide ready access to this material.

4.   Outlines could be developed by study groups for the use of all its members. In this way the work can be divided up and everyone can benefit from the final version.

What Should Be in Your Outline

Clearly, all main concepts should appear in your outline. Chapter titles will most likely become major headings while headings within chapters will appear as subheadings in your general outline. *Don't write too much -- be brief and to the point.* Include examples or applications of concepts in your outline to solidify the concept in your mind. Try to make these examples relate to something with which you are familar. Science is really a description of your world, and formulas learned can be used to explain some occurrence which is part of your experience. *You will be most able to remember concepts which are real to you so select everyday examples of principles if possible.*

Be sure to also incorporate information from your lecture notes. Read both your text and lecture notes as you construct your outline. Include information which was presented in lecture and not included in your text. Your lecturer obviously feels that this material is of special significance, so there is a good chance that it will appear on the exam. Be sure to include it in your general outline. *Graphs, charts, tables or diagrams alluded to in lecture should also be noted in your outline* since they were used by your instructor to demonstrate important points.

As you outline the various topics in your general review, be sure to include information on handouts distributed by the instructor. Handouts require time and energy in their construction, duplication and distribution. If your instructor has invested time and energy in order to provide you with this handout, he or she feels the information it contains is important. Your outline should include and emphasize handout material.

Problems, Problems, and More Problems

Generally, science courses which involve mostly principles and their applications involve large numbers of quantitative problems to solve. These exams primarily consist of solving similar problems. It makes sense to **spend most of your time preparing for this kind of exam by systematically solving problems.** Do the problems associated with the outline. The concepts stressed in the problems should also be incorporated in the outline. Problems are really good indicators of what is important. If you are assigned ten problems on one aspect of a topic and one problem involving another part of the topic, spend more time understanding the concept incorporated in the ten problems. More of your outline should be dedicated to those concepts. Read carefully chapter 5 on Problem Solving in order to review effectively for this type of course.

Category II

Topics Under Review Involving General Principles Along With Numerous Facts

If the subject being studied involves numerous principles and facts which need to be memorized, as in biochemistry, comparative anatomy or pharmacology, then outlining becomes critical in order to make sense of the material. Outlining will connect the principles and various facts so your retention will improve. Trying to memorize facts separately is not only ineffective, but also limits your comprehension of the subject. By seeing facts as parts of general principles, you remember them better, and you understand the principles more clearly.

These outlines, as already indicated, are developed primarily from the text, with embellishments from lecture notes. Material presented in lecture should be included in your outline, and any new material of importance presented in lecture should be added. Your outline is really a combination of textbook and lecture notes along with handouts. Be sure to include important examples presented in the text and the lecture. These will add to your understanding and knowledge of the subject as you review for the exam.

Category III

Topics Under Review Which Involve Mostly Factual Information

For topics which involve categories of similar things, such as classes of drugs which must be memorized in pharmacology, or muscles in anatomy, students find index cards or charts to be particularly helpful. On each index card, or in chart form, list the drugs, for example, which have a similar reaction in the human body and all the important information pertinent to this class of pharmaceuticals. If you need to know a great deal about a particular substance, you can devote an entire index card to this information. This method is effective for course material which lends itself to classes and lists of entities with similar properties. This procedure will help you sort out the numerous facts and organize them in a coherent manner, so that memorization is an easier task. These index cards are particularly helpful when used by study groups.

Example of Index Card Usage

Procainamide

Dynamics:	↓ membrane responsiveness
Kinetics:	20% weakly bound to albumin; renal excretion is greater than hepatic metabolism; N-acetyl DA metabolites: excreted 100% by kidneys $\overline{c}$; with 60% activity of parent careful $\overline{c}$ renal failure
Tx uses:	Suppresses atrial & vent ectopics prevent PSVT or AT FL/FIB Vent. arrhythmias
Sides:	fever SLE like syndrome (30%) Agranulocytosis
Interaction:	relatively free

The words which are underlined in the preceding example can be written on the face of an index card with the information on the other side for self and group testing. This particular index card was used by a medical student studying pharmacology.

Summary of Reviewing Method

Category	Nature of Topic	Method of Review	Most Likely Type of Exam	Example of Subject Containing these Topics
I	Conceptual	Outline	Essay (Problem Solving)	Chemistry, physics, and physiology
II	Conceptual Along with Numerous Facts	Outline for overall principles Index cards, Charts to help memorize facts	Combination of Essay and Objective	Biology, Biochemistry, Organic Chemistry
III	Mostly Memori-zation	Index Cards, Charts	Objective	Anatomy

Time Table For Review

During the first week, decide the best way to review. Construct an outline or make up index cards, depending on the nature of the topics covered by the upcoming exam. Make a study schedule to insure that you spend enough time on all relevant material. If you decide to outline the material, determine the general headings by using your textbook outlines and lecture notes. Decide which topics you will study each week so that you can be sure you will have reviewed all of the work before the exam. Take the following into account when making up this schedule:

1.   Length and complexity of topics

Obviously, if the textbook chapter is lengthy and much lecture time has been devoted to the topic, you need to understand it thoroughly. Make sure a substantial period is devoted to studying this topic. If particular topics are very complex, you may need more time.

2.   How much do you know about the topics already?

If there are concepts or facts which you already know and understand in depth, you don't need much time for their review. Just make sure that you do know them. If there are concepts which you feel you understand, do some problems incorporating them. If there are facts which you think you know well, recite them, and check with your notes. Students often feel confident that they know a topic simply because they understood it at one time. As time goes by, however, this information is usually forgotten. So double-check yourself before you decide to spend a minimum amount of time reviewing a topic, especially one which is clearly important.

Remember that this schedule is approximate. If you find that you have fallen behind because some topics required more time than anticipated, increase the number of hours per week allotted for exam preparation. Try to stick as close to the schedule as possible, so you don't find yourself overloaded with work.

Use of Study Groups

Three weeks before a major exam, continue with your added study time, but also add two to three hours a week to your study group time. Use this time for problems covering exam material in problem solving courses. Each member of the study group can present a series of problems with solutions that cover the important concepts of the course. These problems could be taken from text-books or old exams for the other members of the group to solve. If you can solve the study group problems assigned to you, then you probably know the material. If you are unable to solve the problems, there is usually someone in the group who can explain the solution to you. If you still do not understand the solution, you are made aware of your weaknesses. Make sure you allocate study time to learning the material you don't understand. Each member of the study group should explain the solutions of the problems they solve step by step, and, after explaining the solutions, they should answer any questions from other members of the group.

In courses that require extensive memorization, each member of the study group can develop a series of index cards for use by the entire group. On the front of each card, write the item(s) to be memorized, and, on the back, write all the pertinent information. The cards can be read by a member of the group to the other members. Group members should respond one at a time with the most complete response possible. This not only reviews the material, but also lets you know what you need to study. Study groups can also be used to construct the outlines needed for review. Each member outlines a particular topic. These individual outlines can be combined to produce an outline on all of the material. The group can review each member's work, making changes and additions where appropriate. The final version will be a result of input from everyone in the group.

The Night Before

The final week before a major exam should be a continuation of the previous weeks. You should complete most of your preparation by the night before the exam. In the remaining time before the exam, you should do no more than a quick review of material that is likely to appear on the exam. After that, you should relax, get a good night's sleep, and wake up rested in the morning. Before the exam, have a light meal, as it is important to have something in your stomach when taking an exam. When you arrive at the exam room, proceed immediately into the classroom without talking to other students; sit down and wait for the exam. It is always a bad idea to talk to other students right before an exam, because it is likely to increase anxiety. Students are likely to ask about some topic which you didn't study or a question which you can't answer. Since it is too late to learn the material right before the exam, your anxiety level will rise and affect your peformance. It is interesting to note that, usually, these last minute questions are not relevant to the exam. It is also not a good idea to open your book or review your notes right before an exam. You do not have enough time to effectively study them, and all this will do is lead to confusion.

Suggestions For Successful Test-Taking

Believe it or not, it is not nearly enough to know the material in order to consistently achieve high grades on exams. You must also be aware of effective test-taking techniques in order for exam scores to be accurate reflections of your knowledge.

When taking a major exam, pace yourself. Make sure that you allow yourself enough time to complete all the answers and to go back over your answers. Do not be concerned about how fast other students complete the exam. There is no correlation between the amount of time you need and your success on the exam. Read all the questions completely and carefully. Students reduce their test scores substantially by reading only part of a direction, part of a question, or, on a multiple choice exam, not reading all the answers. Haste on exams will cost you points.

When answering the questions, first answer the ones you know; then answer the ones that you think you know, and finally, attempt to answer the ones that you don't know. This will build confidence and improve your test score. Do not spend too long on any one question. Even if you get the answer correct, you may have used so much time that you will be unable to complete the exam and/or will have to complete it in such a hurry that you will make mistakes. Your exam will not reflect your knowledge of the material. Be aware of point allocation on the exam. Don't spend too much time and effort on questions which are worth only a few points. Spend the most time on those questions or problems which carry the bulk of the points on the exam.

Some Additional Suggestions on Taking and Preparing for Objective and Essay Exams

We have already discussed the general techniques that you should employ when preparing for and taking any major exam. There are also some specific steps you can incorporate into your study pattern which depend on the format of the upcoming exam.

There are two basic types of exams: objective and essay. Let us first discuss an objective examination.

What You Must Know About Objective Exams

An objective examination can consist of any combination of the following types of questions: True/false, multiple choice, multiple multiples, matching, fill in the blank, and short definitions.

Multiple choice items and multiple multiples items contain a number of choices, usually four or five, from which you are expected to choose the correct response. In a multiple choice test, the correct response is the one, best choice. In a multiple multiples test, the correct response will range from none of the choices to all of them. In other words, a multiple multiples test requires that every correct choice be recognized.

An example of multiple multiples is given below. Notice that all possible choices must be considered on this type of test.

Multiple Multiples

Directions: There may be **one** or **more** correct responses to each question. Answer a,b,c,d,e as follows:

a = 1,2,3, correct   b = 1,3 correct
c = 2,4 correct   d = 4 correct
e = all correct.

1. The tunica media _____:
    1. In arterioles is composed of proportionally more smooth muscle than elastic fibers.
    2. In the aorta is composed of proportionally more smooth muscle than elastic fibers.
    3. In arterioles is the tunic to become calcified in old age.
    4. Is the only tunic in capillaries.

2. Veins _____:
    1. Have thinner walls than corresponding arteries.
    2. Have valves.
    3. Have larger lumens than corresponding arteries.
    4. Are double in number compared to arteries.

3. The following statements are correct concerning skin _____:
    1. Epidermis has no vascular supply.
    2. Collagen fibers in the dermis have a prevailing directionality that forms "Langers Lines."
    3. Epidermis is continuously replaced.
    4. The arrector pili muscles are composed of skeletal muscle.

4. The following statements are true regarding digestion **except**:
    a. stomach secretions are acidic
    b. pancreatic secretions include lipase
    c. pancreatic secretions are acidic
    d. stomach secretions include mucus

5. Bile is a complex solution containing:
    a. Bile salts, cholesterol, pigments
    b. Bile salts, lecithin, HCl
    c. Bile salts, pigments, carboxy peptidase
    d. None of these combinations

There are two types of matching questions shown below.

Matching Column

Directions: Match each numbered item with a given letter in the column at the right. A given letter may be used more than once.

28.	Typical urine pH	a.	5 vol. %
29.	Arterial pO_2	b.	26mM/liter
30.	O_2 content of mixed venous blood	c.	40mm Hg
31.	Minimum urine pH	d.	5.0
32.	Arterial HCO_3 concentration	e.	46 mm Hg
33.	Typical urine osmolarity	f.	15 ml O2/100 ml blood
35.	Venous pCO_2	h.	6.0
36.	Major form in which CO_2 is transported in blood	i.	300 mOsm/liter
37.	Minimum urine osmolarity	j.	50 mOsm/liter
38.	Venous pO_2	k.	none of these

Directions: Match each numbered item with a given letter from the column at the right. Use each given letter only once.

39.	chief cells	a.	stomach
40.	haustra	b.	colon
41.	islets of Langerhans	c.	pancreas
42.	Peyers patches	d.	ileum
43.	Brunner's glands	e.	duodenum

An example of fill in the blanks items is shown below.

Fill in the Blanks

Answer "increase", "decrease" or "no change"

1. A rise in hematocrit leads to a(an) _____ in blood flow through a particular region.

2. A(an) _____ in tissue pO_2 leads to vasodilation in the pulmonary circulation.

3. A(an) _____ in tissue pCO_2 leads to vasodilation in the cerebral circulation.

4.   An increase in firing from carotid or aortic baroreceptors leads to
        a reflex _____ in a sympathetic discharge from the vasomotor
        center.

An example of a true/false question is shown below.

True/False
        A -ΔG means a spontaneous process.

When studying for an objective exam, use the methodology described
previously, but in addition, focus on the kinds of questions that you will be
asked. Objective exams focus on specific bits of information. When you are
studying for an objective examination, focus on the specific points that the textbook and classroom notes have emphasized throughout the course.

With an objective exam, practicing will greatly improve your score. If you
know that many multiple choice questions will appear on the exam, then you
should develop for your study group and your own use a large number of
multiple choice questions. Use old exams and quizzes with multiple choice
questions. If the exam will include many matching questions, develop a large
number of matching questions. Put yourself in the instructor's shoes. Try to
ask the kinds of questions you think will be asked. By developing objective
questions of your own, you will not only get valuable practice, but the
development of these kinds of questions will more clearly define the material that
you have to study.

The defining of terms in an objective examination is a special case. Definitions
are different from most other forms of objective examination because the answer
is not already there for you; you must provide it. They are a special case
because you can guarantee yourself one hundred percent on this part of an
objective examination. All you have to do is learn all the definitions that have
been covered in the lecture, handouts and the textbook. Make sure that you
don't simply memorize these definitions, but that you understand them. If you
simply memorize them, you are far more likely to forget them when you are
under the pressure of taking an exam than if you really understand them.

When taking an objective exam, it is very important to read the instructions
carefully. Students often lose points by misreading the instructions or reading
only part of the instructions. Read each specific question completely. Make
sure that you understand what you are being asked. In multiple choice
questions, read all the answers before choosing one. Students frequently lose
points by picking the first answer which seems appropriate. If they had read all
the answers, they would have discovered that there was a more appropriate
answer.

When taking an objective exam, it is extremely important that you pace yourself. If you have fifty questions and an hour to complete them, this means that you have a minute per question and ten minutes to check them. Do not spend too long on any one question. Even if you get the answer correct, you may have wasted so much time that you will either be unable to complete the exam or forced to complete it in such a hurry that you will make careless mistakes.

Answer the questions which you know first. Then, answer questions you think you know, and, finally try the ones you don't know at all. This will build your confidence and thus improve your score.

Find out if there is a penalty for guessing on the exam. If there is no penalty, then it pays to guess where you do not know the answer. On a multiple choice question, you can greatly improve your success at guessing by eliminating answers that you know are incorrect. Often, on a multiple choice question where you are not sure of the answer, you can eliminate several answers that you know are incorrect, and increase your chances of getting the correct answer. The time to do this is not while you are taking the exam, but only after you have finished and are reviewing it.

When guessing on **true/false** questions you can also improve your odds. Look for qualifying words such as *most of the time* or *often*. Statements like this tend to be true. On the other hand, statements that say *always* or *never* are more often false, because one exception to the statement would make them false.

When you are doing **matching questions**, you will increase your odds of matching the ones you don't know if you first eliminate the ones that you do know. It is also important to know whether a matching answer can be used more than once or only once. In situations where answers can only be used once, you are much more likely to guess correctly than in a situation where an answer can be used more than once.

On **multiple multiples**, you can often get the answer to the first question by reading the questions that are based on that first question. Usually, the followup questions will give you considerable information about the first question, and sometimes, they will even give you the answer.

On **fill in the blank** and **short definitions**, it is always better to put something in than to have no answer at all. On fill in the blank, even if the answer you have in mind does not fit into the space, put it down anyway. There is often little relationship between the answer and the size of the space left for it. When you are defining something, even if you cannot remember the exact definition, you should put down anything that you can remember about what you are defining. You may receive partial credit.

When you go back over your exam, in addition to answering the questions that you had not previously answered, you also should correct questions that you have mistakenly answered. Be careful when you change an answer on an objective exam. Usually, on an objective examination, your first answer will be the correct one, and you will change your answer from a correct answer to an incorrect one. So, unless you are absolutely sure that your first answer was wrong and your new answer is correct, don't make any changes.

There is one major exception to this rule: short definitions. Usually, if you go back over your short definitions, the corrections you make will improve your answers rather than detract from them. Use the time you have after completing your exam to tighten up your definitions so they are clear and concise. Sometimes, you may need to change the definition completely, realizing that you misunderstood the term the first time you read it. The corrections and changes that you make will usually improve your answer.

Essay Exams

The second major type of exam is an essay exam. There are two basic types of essay exams; the familiar written essay exam and the mathematical essay. We will begin by discussing the written essay exam.

While there are many similarities between preparing for a written essay exam and an objective exam, there are some very important differences. Essay exams focus on general concepts. When studying for an essay examination, spend most of your time studying the general concepts. You must first identify what these concepts are, and then, make sure that you understand them. Make sure you include the important concepts that have been covered in lecture, by the textbook, and handouts in the outline you construct as you review the material. Turn each one of these concepts into an essay type exam question using such words as *describe the following* or *explain the following*. Then, answer the questions you have just written. Your review should always keep the exam in mind. As you review each topic, ask yourself questions in essay form to be sure you understand the material sufficiently for the exam. Use old exams or quizzes or questions taken from other textbooks to aid you in preparing for the exam.

When answering these questions, first answer them in your head. Think out the answer before putting it on paper. If possible, make an outline of the answer before you write it. It is important when you are answering these practice questions to answer them in the most complete, concise and well organized manner possible.

Bring essay type questions to your study group and have different members of the group attempt to answer them. Compare your answers with theirs. The responses should look fairly similar. When answering these questions, imitate test conditions as closely as possible. That means close your textbook and notebooks, do not talk to the rest of the members of the study group, and impose a time limit on how long you have to answer the questions. By practicing taking essay exams, you will reduce your anxiety about the exam and improve your ability to create a well organized and well structured answer to essay questions on the exam. Usually, by doing what we have suggested, you will be able to approximate what will be on the examination.

When you take a written essay exam, be sure to allocate your time very carefully. Make sure you leave enough time at the end of the examination to go over your answers. Answer the questions you are sure about first, then go back and answer the questions you think you know, and finally, attempt the ones you do not know at all.

It is important when answering a written essay question to organize your answer carefully. Be clear and concise. Before you write your answer, make an outline in your head. This will strengthen your answer and add points to your score. Do not make the mistake that many students do in believing that the longest answer is the best answer. Do not throw in information in the hope that it might have some relationship to the question. Doing either of these things will cost you points. Remember, a well organized and concise answer is the best answer.

After you have finished answering the questions, leave plenty of time to go over the answers. Use this time to weed out irrelevant points and add important points which you had omitted previously. You can gain a lot of points on an essay examination this way.

What about the short answer essay type question? Studying for an exam that will have many short answer questions is similar to studying for a written essay exam. The major difference is in your focus when studying.

We said earlier that objective examinations usually require the studying of specific points and essay examinations require the studying of general concepts. Short answer essay questions require studying of **midrange** concepts. Those ideas that help explain the general concepts and are usually illustrated by specific examples are what we call midrange concepts. In most other respects, studying for a short answer exam follows the same rules as studying for a written essay exam. If you outline your textbook and classroom notes, you will usually find that general concepts are the roman numerals, midrange concepts are the capitalized letters under the roman numerals, and specific points are the arabic numbers under the capitalized letters.

Exams on Solving Problems

A second major type of essay question is the mathematical essay question. This is any test question that requires calculation through the use of formulas. We define these as essay questions for two reasons; 1) in order to answer these questions, you must understand the general concepts in a subject area and 2) many of the same study skills and techniques required for a written essay must be employed when studying for an exam using formulas and relationships to solve problems. There are, however, some special techniques that need to be used when preparing for a problem solving exam. It is important to solve all the problems that are given as samples in your textbook and in lecture. Read carefully the chapter on Problem Solving in order to prepare adequately for the exam. In addition, use your study group during the semester and divide up all the problems at the end of each chapter among members of the study group. Bring the solutions to the next study group session so you can explain the answers to each other. Make sure you record every step of the solution clearly. It is also a good idea to develop additional problems and solve them. They can be taken from other textbooks, past exams or quizzes. The more problems you solve, the more you will know the material, and your exam performance will improve. Right before the exam, you might have the study group develop a practice exam which each member of the group should take under exam-like conditions. This exercise is extremely beneficial since it helps you become desensitized to exam conditions. Many students fall below their potential because of the anxiety they experience during exams By practicing solving problems under test conditions, you lessen your anxiety and your performance will more closely reflect your understanding of the material.

When you are studying for an exam that will require the use of formulas and equations, make sure that you understand the formulas and equations and do not simply memorize them. (See Chapter 5 on Problem Solving.) It is important particularly with formulas, to understand that each formula explains a piece of reality. Then, you know exactly what systems it applies to and what it says about this system. Students who memorize formulas and equations often run into trouble on exams. Many formulas describe similar but not identical situations. If you are not sure when a relationship is applicable, chances are you will use it inappropriately on exams.

When you are solving problems during exams, underline the important data when you first read the problem. All given data should be underlined, as well as what you are being asked to solve. Important words which describe the system or process should be highlighted as well. For almost all topics in the sciences, a special vocabulary must be learned. This will become apparent to you as you solve the problems in your text. Make note of these recurring terms, and be sure you clearly understand their meaning. It is helpful to look for and underline these key terms and phrases when they appear in problems as well. Solutions will become more apparent when you understand the specific vocabulary used in problems.

Use the four step approach to problem solving described in Chapter 5 on Problem Solving. Clearly list the given information including units; indicate what you are solving for; plan your solution, and then, check your answer.

When you are solving problems on an exam, make sure you clearly show your work. Many instructors will take off points, even if your answer is correct, unless all of the work is included. By taking pains to include all of the steps you used in your solution, you also increase your chances of receiving partial credit, in case some of these steps were wrong. By clearly showing your solution, you maximize your chances of receiving credit for what you know. Writing down all of the steps you take in solving a problem helps you to see your own errors. You can pick up on mistakes more easily when you can examine your solution in detail.

Always use a calculator for arithmetic operations. Don't waste time dividing, multiplying, taking logs etc. Check the batteries in your calculator before the exam and bring in some extras just in case. Don't take a chance on wasting time during exams by doing arithmetic. Make sure your calculator is functional and includes all of the operations which you might require. Always check the reasonableness of an answer. If you are solving for the weight of a person and your answer is 15,000 kg, you have made an error. Remember, science is about your world, so don't leave your common sense outside the exam room. If you are solving for an unknown such as bond energy, think of other bond energies with which you have worked to get some ideas about reasonable values. Make sure your units are correct. Double check that you solved for the unknown in the problem. Students often solve for a different unknown simply because they solved for this unknown in past exams. In deciding your answer, reread the problem and make sure you have the right unknown.

What happens if you are sure your answer is incorrect? Recheck your arithmetic with your calculator. You may have omitted an arithmetic operation or used the wrong values of the given information. By using scientific notations, i.e., values expressed as exponents, you can easily see if the mistakes are just arithmetic. If not, look at the relationships you've used, and make sure they apply to the system given in the problem. If you are not sure that they do, think of some others which might apply, and redo the problem. Think of problems you have solved which are similar. Do you know of other relationships which involve the given variables and unknowns?

Examine the given information carefully. In many cases, other data can be easily obtained from the given data. For example, if the density and volume of a liquid are known, the mass of that sample of liquid is known as well.

$$(d = \frac{mass}{volume} \qquad mass = d \times volume).$$

By recognizing that the mass is known, you may be able to see some connection between given information and your unknown.

Post Exam Period

When an exam is returned, do not simply look at the grade and then forget about the exam. Carefully go over the exam and note your errors. See where you made your mistakes. It is important to correct your mistakes and make sure that you now understand the concepts that you did not understand previously. If you are unable to understand why your answers were incorrect or how you made the mistake, ask the professor to explain the question to you. Think about why you answered the question or problem incorrectly. How could you have improved your preparation so that these mistakes may have been avoided?

Learning in the sciences is a building block process. You must lay a strong foundation or you will never fully understand the material. The learning of new material is based on the material that you have already learned. An exam helps you to know what you have learned fully and what you have not. The exam is your guide to where you are strong and where you are weak. Therefore, it is very important that you use the exam as a way to strengthen your weaknesses so when you take the next exam, you will have laid the foundation that you need to be successful in the sciences.

Five
Problem-Solving Techniques: A Systematic Approach

Problem solving is such a common practice in our lives that we often are unaware of when and how we solve the problems we confront. Students often only realize that they are solving problems when they do assigned problems from the back of a chapter of a text or when taking an exam, although we all are constantly solving problems of one kind or another. The patterns and skills we develop in one area of our lives affect the way we approach problems in general; if we develop effective problem solving skills in the sciences, for example, they will be carried over not only into other subjects, but also into the way we deal with everyday problems.

Some people think that superior problem solving skills develop from inborn talent only and cannot be acquired. Recent research (C.T. Metles, A. Pilot, H. Roossink, and H. Kramer Pals, *J. Chem. Ed.*, 57, 883 1980), however, contradicts that notion; effective problem solving processes can be learned by applying a systematic approach to problems of increasing degrees of difficulty. Once a problem has been solved and thoroughly understood, a specific pattern is formed and problem-solving capabilities are strengthened. More difficult problems can be solved. Problem solving skills are learned by systematically working at solving problems.

We discuss some special study techniques which help improve your problem solving ability. These techniques will aid you in acquiring the information you need to solve problems. We also present an analytical systematic procedure which will guide your thinking towards reaching solutions. Initially, you will need to follow the procedure closely. As your problem solving ability improves, however, you will find that you are automatically following the procedure. There is no short cut method for developing problem solving skills; what we offer you here are steps you can take and procedures you can follow to become a more effective problem solver.

The more you apply our guidelines to your work and to the problems assigned, the more skilled you will become at finding solutions. The benefits you derive will depend on the amount of time and energy you expend in their acquisition.

Special Study Techniques

Before you can begin to solve a problem, you must acquire necessary information and understand the material. Chapters 2 and 3 on effective text-book reading and lecture note-taking skills will be helpful in constructing this data bank upon which you will need to draw. There are also some special techniques which are particularly useful when preparing to solve a problem.

Look at Problems Assigned Before Reading the Chapter

It's a good idea to read the assigned problems at the end of the chapter before you begin reading. If you do so, you will have some knowledge of the variables with which you will be working and what kinds of systems you'll need to understand. As a result, you will pay close attention to the material discussing these variables.

Carefully Read and Understand Sample Problems

It is important to thoroughly understand sample problems, because they highlight important concepts in the chapter. When you look at a sample problem try to understand the steps taken in finding a solution; ask yourself the following questions:

> What principle or principles is the problem demonstrating?
> What information given in the problem suggested that this principle
>   was involved?
> Why was each calculation performed?
> How does this sample problem differ from others given?

After you can answer these questions, try to do the problem yourself. Take a sheet of paper, and solve the problem without looking at the text. You might even change the values given, so you can be sure you have not simply memorized the solution of the sample problem. When you work problems assigned at the end of the chapter or given on an exam, keep these sample problems in mind. They often will lead to solutions, because they stress concepts which appear in many problems. Make note of problems presented by the instructor. Since time and effort was expended in discussing the problem, it must be important to the instructor and should be understood thoroughly. After lecture, when reviewing notes, do the problem on your own. Think of how the question might appear on an exam. Are there sample problems or assigned problems in the text that are similar to the lecture problems? Work these problems out to make sure you understand the concepts involved.

Categorize Problems

Problems which cover similar topics very often use similar approaches and concepts. In studying sample problems in particular, make note of the topic and the steps that are followed in reaching a solution. Identify the terms and phrases in the problem which indicate the topic and look for these keys when solving new problems. As an example, examine the two problems provided below. Note how both involve application of PV = nRT.

Examples
from *Fundamentals of Chemistry*, Frank Brescia, John Arents, Herbert Meislich, and Amos Turk: Academic Press, 1980. p.79.

Example I
A bicycle tire containing 0.406 mol of air will burst when its internal pressure reaches 7.25 atm. at which time its internal volume will be 1.52 liters. To what temperature must the air in the tube be heated to cause a blowout?

Quantities given: $n = 0.406$ mol
                      $P = 7.25$ atm.
                      $V = 1.52$ L
Quantity sought: T
Therefore we must solve PV = nRT for T

Example II
The explorations of the Martian atmosphere have revealed that its temperature can be as high as 27°C at the equator at noon. Its surface pressure is about 8 torr. If a spacecraft could collect $10m^3$ of this atmosphere, compress it to a small volume, and send it back to Earth, how many moles would the sample contain?

Quantities given: $P = 8$ torr
                      $V = 10$ m
                      $T = 27$ C
Quantity sought: n
Therefore we must solve PV = nRT for n

As you work through problems on specific topics, make note of the concepts, formulas and assumptions that continually recur. Make associations between the system or process described in the problem and the scientific principles which are applied. It will become apparent that the same principles recur. In most cases, you will be unable to review all of the problems related to topics being covered on an upcoming exam. If you categorize problems, you can choose one or two problems to review for each class so that your review is thorough. Asterisk problems which you know are important as you study for a course. Be sure to understand these problems when you review for an exam.

Formulas and Problem Solving

To many students, formulas are just mathematical relationships which must be memorized and used to solve problems by substituting given values. Formulas are viewed as esoteric, algebraic expressions which generate answers to problems. As a result, students frequently apply the formulas inappropriately since they have only a superficial understanding of the meaning of the formulas they memorize. It is important to remember that formulas are concise mathematical statements about some system or process in the real world. They describe how things change around us. To understand these relationships thoroughly you need to think about:

a) What system or process in the world does it describe?
b) What does it say about the system or process?
c) How can it be applied?

Only by spending time thinking appropriately about each formula can you really begin to understand it sufficiently to apply it to problems with success. For example, Henry's Law which is used in biology, chemistry, physics, and physiology relates pressure of a gas (A) above a solution to concentration of the gas in solution.

$$P_A = k_H x_A$$

P_A = partial pressure of gas A

k_H = Henry's Law constant at a temperature T and for a specific solute solvent system.

x_A = mole fraction of A in solution

If you are studying this formula you must think about the following:
a) What does Henry's Law describe?
It describes a system involving a gas A above a solution and the amount of A dissolved in the solution.

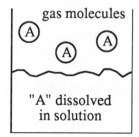

b)   What does Henry's law say about this system?

Pressure of A above solution is directly proportional to amount in solution. If pressure of A increases, more will dissolve in solution. If P_A decreases, amount in solution will decrease.

c)   How can it be applied?

Knowing the partial pressure and k_H you can determine amount of A in solution. For example, you could calculate the amount of O_2 or N_2 dissolved in blood by knowing P_{O_2} and P_{N_2} in the lungs. By knowing one variable, you can easily determine the other.

d)   Can you think of everyday applications of this formula?

Opening a soda causes gas to escape. CO_2 is dissolved in soda under high P_{CO_2}. When can is opened P_{CO_2} is very small and CO_2 comes out of solution.

This system of self-questioning is essential if you are going to achieve the level of understanding necessary to solve problems. It is especially important if you are overwhelmed with many formulas in your courses. You need to take the time to think about the formulas, so you can clearly distinguish between them, know when they apply, and know what they mean.

To help you accomplish this goal, it is a good idea to develop a Key Relations Chart for each major topic. Not only will the construction of the chart be useful in really learning the formulas, but also, it will serve as a review of the important relationships for exams. Even if you don't construct a chart, use the guidelines described to study formulas.

This chart which you will develop must at least include:

a)   List of the important relationships

b)   Description of each variable and constant which appears in the formula along with appropriate units.

c)   Description of the system and/or process which the formula is about.

d)   What the formula can be used for? Give some examples, especially those which involve things you are familiar with.

By writing down this information, you are thinking about each formula and really learning it. What you don't understand will become apparent during this process, and you can consult your text, lecture or textbook notes, or ask the instructor or a classmate in your study group. Finding out what you don't understand before an exam is clearly preferable to making this discovery during an exam.

Following is a Key Relations Chart involving some basic scientific relationships on work and energy. These simple formulas are used throughout chemistry and physics and are necessary for some biological fields as well. Note the column format that is used. Following this format helps you think systematically and thoroughly about each formula making sure your understanding is complete. As already indicated, these charts will help you prepare for exams, especially final exams which encompass massive amounts of material.

Relationship	Meaning of Variables and Units	Description of Formula and Applications
$F = mg$	F = force (push or pull) newtons m = mass (-kg) g = gravitational acceleration $= 9.8$ m/sec2	F = downward gravitational force exerted on a mass m by the earth (same as weight)
$F = \dfrac{Gm_1 m_2}{r^2}$	r = distance between m_1 and m_2 G = gravitational constant = $6.672 \times 10^{-11} \dfrac{m^3}{kg\ sec^2}$	F = attractive gravitational force between two bodies m_1 and m_2 If m_1 = mass of earth then $F = m_2 g$ and $g = \dfrac{Gm_1}{r^2}$
$w = f\ x\ r$	w = work (Joules) r = distance over which force acts.	Work is done when a force is exerted over a distance. If work is done on an object the energy of object may increase
$PE = mgh$	PE = potential energy (Joules) h = height to which body m is lifted	PE of a body increases when h increases -- work done on body by lifting.
$KE = \dfrac{1}{2} mv^2$	KE = Kinetic Energy -- energy of motion V = velocity m/sec	Form of energy can be changed into PE.

Some Pitfalls About Understanding Formulas

In developing your chart, try to keep formulas describing similar systems or processes together. That will help you get a more complete picture of these systems or processes. It will also help you see the difference between them, making use of the wrong formula in problem solving less likely.

In some cases, several related formulas are presented, i.e. they are specific cases of the same relationship. For example, the Ideal Gas Law $PV = nRT$ will yield Boyles Law $PV = k_t$ under conditions of constant T (isothermal) and Charles Law $\frac{V}{T} = k_p$ when the pressure is held constant (isobaric). List these three formulas together, indicating their relationship. By making note of their relationship, it becomes unnecessary for you to know all three, since Boyle's and Charles' Laws are just specific cases of $PV = nRT$. Try to minimize the amount of material you need to memorize by understanding the **main relationship** and deriving others by applying this main relationship to specific cases. Another advantage to studying formulas in this way is that you will not lose sight of the general principle. Frequently, when students are confronted with several related formulas, they have difficulty recognizing the underlying principle. Typically, the wrong formula is applied to a problem because the general principle became buried under the mass of related formulas.

In developing your chart and seeking to understand formulas, make sure you describe the constants used in formulas and their associated units. Indicate if they change with different conditions. This is important since there are numerous constants used in science, some of which use the same letters, so its particularly important to separate them out and know when they are applicable. The units of constants match with other units in the formula, so by reviewing units of the constants, you are also reviewing the **appropriate** units used in the formulas.

Four-Step Approach To Problem Solving

Solving a problem successfully involves following an analytical, systematic procedure. The steps of this procedure will be described below with examples. Following this systematic procedure will improve your problem solving skills, as it will help you to read problems carefully, identify important values, and apply analytical reasoning.

At the end of this chapter, there are worksheets which you can use to practice the technique described on problems of your choice. Use them and practice frequently. You will find that you will begin to follow the steps listed below automatically when presented with a problem.

1.   Analyze the problem.
2.   Develop a plan for solving the problem.
3.   Perform the appropriate calculations.
4.   Evaluate your answer.

Step 1 -- Problem Analysis

When analyzing a problem, it is generally very helpful to diagram the process or system described in the problem. In this way, you will be able to see at a glance

what the problem is about. The time you spend drawing the diagram will be more than made up for, since re-reading the problem over and over will no longer be necessary. In the diagram, you should indicate the given values and their associated units. Each value should be labeled clearly, so there is no doubt as to what it represents.

The unknown should be labeled as well and, if possible, its units. In some cases, it is a good idea to immediately define the unknown since its definition may indicate that first another variable must be determined before the unknown can be calculated. If you are aware of the variable that you must calculate at the beginning, you should be able to formulate an appropriate plan for solving the problem.

Step 2 -- Develop a Plan

Before doing any calculations, you should plan out the solution. Doing calculations without thinking the problem through generates more data, making the solution even more difficult to find.

In planning the solution, think of relationships and formulas which link up the unknown and the given data. It's generally best to work backwards, selecting equations which involve the unknown, and see if they can be combined with the given data to solve the problem. Look for additional given data if you cannot immediately see the solution. For example, since $F = ma$, if both a and m are provided, then F is also known. Including F as given data may lead to the solution to the problem.

Step 3 -- Perform Required Calculations

Before substituting numerical values into an equation, it's a good idea to derive a relationship for the unknown, then insert the appropriate values and perform the necessary calculations. Check the units of each value carefully, making sure the units are all in the same unit system: MKS (SI), CGS, or the English unit system. Make any conversion necessary before performing the calculation. Use a calculator for all arithmetic operations, combining steps to save time. Store values which are used repeatedly in a calculation such as π.

MKs = meter, kg, sec   CGS = cm, gram, sec   English = ft, slug, sec

Step 4 -- Evaluate Your Answer

After you have calculated an answer, make sure it's the one the problem asks for; check your analysis where you indicated the unknown and compare. Ask yourself if your answer is reasonable. If, for example, you've calculated the height of a building as 10^6 m, you've made an error and should check your solution. If your answer involves a quantity such as free energy, and you're not sure how reasonable your answer is, compare it to values you've seen in the text or in lecture. Check the units of your answer and the number of significant figures. Points are generally deducted on exams when either units are not included or incorrect, or when the wrong number of significant figures are present. Even more importantly, incorrect units indicate an error in your plan, and you must go back and formulate another plan to solve the problem correctly.

In the problems worked out below, note the self help questions which help you complete each step. The questions for the plan stage are designed to help you focus in on the relationships which are relevant to the problem at hand. The plan stage is really the most difficult in finding a solution. You must sift through all of the material you have studied and isolate the information which is needed. Asking yourself the right questions will lead you to the pertinent relationships. Use the work sheets provided to apply the four step approach to problems assigned in your courses. After working out a number of problems, the steps will become automatic and your problem solving ability will improve.

Sample Problem

Calculate the kinetic energy of a 1680 kg car travelling at 80 km/hr.

Analysis	Solution	Self-Questions
	$m = 1680$ kg	
		What is known about this system or process?
	80 km/hr.	
	Kinetic Energy	What are we being asked to find?

KE = energy of motion   Define or describe unknown

$$\text{and } KE = \frac{1}{2} mv^2$$

Plan

What relationship(s) involves
the unknown?

$$KE = \frac{1}{2} mv^2$$

Which of these also involve
given information?

Calculation

$$m = 1680 \text{ kg}$$

$$v = \left(80 \frac{\text{km}}{\text{hr}}\right)\left(1000 \frac{\text{m}}{\text{km}}\right)\left(\frac{1 \text{ hr}}{3600 \text{ sec.}}\right) = 22\frac{\text{m}}{\text{s}}$$

$$KE = \frac{1}{2}(1680\text{kg})(22\frac{\text{m}}{\text{s}})^2 = 4.1 \times 10^5 \text{J}$$

Substitute appropriate values.
Make sure units are in the right unit system.
Do all necessary conversions before calculating unknown.

Answer Check

Yes (Kinetic Energy)   Have you answered the
                              problem? (see unknown in
                              analysis.)

Yes (Joule is SI)   Are units correct?
unit for energy

Compare with KE's   Is your answer reasonable?
of other systems that
you calculated or were
given in the text or in
lecture.

Yes (see section on   Does your answer have the
Significant Figures)   correct number of figures?

Worksheet 1

Problem:	Self-Questions
Analysis	Diagram process or system described.
	What is known about this system or process? (Include units and describe fully any given values.)
	What is the unknown? (Include units) Define or describe unknown.
Plan	What relationship(s) involves the unknown? Which of these relationships also involve given information?
	Can values which are not directly supplied be calculated from the given data?
Calculation	Substitute appropriate values.
	Make sure units are in the right unit system.
Answer Check	Have you answered the problem? (See analysis)
	Are units correct?
	Is your answer reasonable?
	Do you have the right number of significant figures?

Worksheet 2

Problem	Self-Questions
Analysis	Diagram process or system described.
	What is known about this system or process? (Include units and describe fully any given values.)
	What is the unknown? (Include units) Define or describe unknown.
Plan	What relationship(s) involves the unknown? Which of these relationships also involve given information?
	Can values which are not directly supplied be calculated from the given data?
Calculation	Substitute appropriate values.
	Make sure units are in the right unit system.
Answer Check	Have you answered the problem? (See analysis)
	Are units correct?
	Is your answer reasonable?
	Do you have the right number of significant figures?

Where, Why, and How You Can Go Wrong

After grading thousands of exams in science courses, we have observed recurring errors made by students seeking solutions to problems on exams. In the chart below, we have listed common mistakes, indicated where they occur in the four-step approach, and specifically how they can be avoided. It is a good idea for you to practice doing problems and use this chart to analyze your work.

Mistake	Stage	Possible Explanation	How to Avoid Mistakes
Solved for the wrong variable	Analysis	Problem similar to other problems studied which involved a different unknown.	Read problem carefully-- Don't assume what the problem asks for. Check units.
	Answer check	Several variables in problem with same units	Label variables more completely if units are the same.
Wrong formula used	Plan	Did not plan out solution but started to solve immediately.	Follow procedure.
		Did not study formulas thoroughly.	Construct Key Relations Chart.
Formula incorrectly written	Plan	Did not study from a Key Relations Chart.	Construct a Key Relations Chart.
Wrong numerical answer	Calculation	Substituted wrong values. Mistake in arithmetical manipulations.	Carefully record known values in analysis and use these for your calculations. Be sure answer is reasonable. If not first check math.
	Answer check		
Wrong units	Plan	Did not study formulas carefully. Must know units of all variables.	Construct a Key Relations Chart.

A Systematic Approach to Problem Solving: Summary

Four Steps

1.   Analysis

    a)   Diagram system or process described in problem.
    b)   Indicate given data and units.
    c)   Indicate unknown and units.
    d)   Define unknown if necessary.

2.   Plan the Solution to Problem

    a)   Consult Key Relation chart and locate relationships involving known and unknown.

    b)   Best to work backwards; start with relationships involving unknown.

    c)   Reduce problem to one equation and one unknown or number of equations = number of unknowns.

3.   Perform Algebraic Calculations

    a)   Plug in values -- make sure units are correct.

4.   Check Answer

    a)   Have you determined the unknown in Ic?

    b)   Is your value reasonable? Check units.

Some Other Helpful Hints on Problem Solving

If you believe that your answer is incorrect, you should check your calculations. The most likely place for students to make an error in problem solving is in their mathematical calculations. Put down every step clearly when solving a problem, so you can find mistakes easily. Use a calculator when performing arithmetic operations. This eliminates one source of error. If, after checking your calculations, you find that you have not made a mathematical error, question the formula(s) you used. Was it the appropriate formula(s)?

Make sure that the relationships you've used are relevant to the system or process described in the problem. In many cases, students use an incorrect formula because it contains a variable that appears to be appropriate but pertains to an entirely different system. For example, X, which generally indicates mole fraction, appears in many formulas. In some formulas, it means mole fraction of gases, while in others, it pertains to mole fraction in solution. The two systems are different, so if you are calculating X in solution, you cannot solve for X in a formula associated with gases. Try to avoid this error by making sure the relationship(s) you apply involve the same system presented in the problem. If, after looking over the relationships you used, you are still unsure why it was the incorrect one, check your basic assumptions about the problem.

We make assumptions because they seem to flow logically from the problem we are solving. Usually, these assumptions are correct, but not always. When your initial assumptions about a problem do not prove adequate to solve a problem, then these assumptions must be questioned. Sometimes, it helps to try to look at the problem in a different way than you did the first time. Many times, formulas are inappropriately used because the problem appears similar to other problems and students make similar assumptions. Be alert to this tendency; although thinking about how other problems were solved is helpful, don't memorize the solutions and apply them carelessly. Typically, new problems involve similar concepts but different conditions, so the relevant formulas change.

If, having taken these steps, you still cannot solve the problem, read the problem again. Often, students put limitations into the problem that simply do not exist. These limitations can make it difficult or impossible to solve the problem. Students also leave out limitations in the problem that do exist and this, too, can result in obtaining the wrong solution.

Usually, you will be able to locate your error in one of the above ways. If you cannot, it is a good idea to bring the problem to your study group. Either someone else in the study group will have found a solution to it, or as a group, you can try to solve the problem collectively.

Six
How to Form and Use a Study Group Effectively

Many students do all their studying alone. They believe that this is the most effective way to learn their assigned material. While we also believe that students often need to study alone, much studying, particularly, the review portion of studying, can be accomplished more effectively in a group situation.

Let us begin by defining what we mean by a study group. A group consists of three to five students. This group should not consist of classmates which might hinder the studying process. It is advisable to avoid close friends in your study group. Select students who are serious about their classwork and attend class well-prepared.

A study group must meet on a regular basis to be effective. We suggest once a week. Except when preparing for a major exam, sessions should last for two to three hours. Group members must have specific tasks to complete before coming to the study group session, and the study group must have an agenda of what it plans to complete while the group is convening. This will guard against one of the basic weaknesses of a study group: not knowing what to do and therefore wasting time.

What are the tasks best suited for a study group?

1.   The study group meeting is an ideal time to review lecture notes. During the course of each lecture, there are usually one or more statements made by the professor which you either missed completely or are unclear about. While it is possible that an individual might miss something vital in a lecture, it is extremely unlikely that all the members of a study group would miss an important point. It is a good idea before the study group meets for everybody in the group to make copies of their classroom notes for the rest of the study group. Sharing your classroom notes has a second advantage; in addition to filling in topic areas where your notes are weak or non existent, it allows you to check whether your notes are capturing the important topics in the lecture at all. All members of the study group should have notes that are similar. If your notes are completely different from everybody else's, you are taking poor lecture notes. Since you are in a study group with other students, they can help you improve your note taking capabilities.

2.   Another important task of a study group is to review the textbook together. This means that you must have read the textbook before you come to study group. In courses where you are outlining the textbook, the outline must have been completed before your study group meets; it is a good idea to make copies for the rest of the study group. In those few courses where the volume of material dictates that you must underline the textbook, that task also should be completed before your study group convenes. Make note of whatever is unclear in your text, so you can ask members of the group about this material. Your questions will benefit others as well, since most likely another member is uncertain about this same material.

3.   Problems or questions which are assigned should be reviewed by the study group. Assignments can be divided up so that each member is responsible for completing specific problems. The solutions can then be reviewed by the group, and pertinent questions can be answered.

4.   An important task of a study group is to help prepare for a major exam. At least four weeks before a major exam, study group meetings should be increased by about two hours a

week. This additional time should be used solely to study for the exam. If the exam is in a problem solving course such as Chemistry or Physics, this time should be primarily allocated to problem solving. Each member of the study group should be required to create five to ten problems with solutions each week on material that has been studied in the course. Other members of the group can select problems at random to solve. These solutions can then be explained to the groupas a whole. If problems cannot be successfully completed, the student who developed the problems should present and explain the solutions. This kind of review is excellent practice for a major exam. Previous exams also make excellent exercises for exam preparation.

If the course consists largely of memorization of material or requires structural location, such as general Biology and Zoology, each student should be asked to develop questions that other students can answer. Since much of the information for the exam will have to be located visually, visual illustration should accompany the questions. Once the questions have been distributed, the same format should be used for answering them, as in the case of the problem solving science courses. Many science courses require a combination of problem solving and memorization, such as Genetics and Physiology. In this case, the study group should develop both problem based questions and non problem based questions.

Forming a study group can often be difficult, and making one work can be even harder. Students who do not know each other may feel uncomfortable about the idea of working together. At some campuses, students commute from many different places. Often, if you want to work in a study group, you will have to initiate the formation of that group. The best place for the study group to meet may be right on campus, a location that the whole group will have in common. Even if students feel uncomfortable about forming a study group, you may be convinced to try at least once. If you follow the suggestions made above, the experience of the first study group meeting should convince these doubters to return.

It is extremely important to meet on a regular basis. For a study group to work most effectively, it must be used to working together. It is also important that members of the group do their fair share of the work. Students who come to the group unprepared or underprepared should be dropped from the group if they continue to come without having completed their work. The group must work as a team and all members of the team must participate equally. A well run study group is an enormous asset to students in science and medical programs. The study group will have a major impact on your success as a science or medical student.

Seven
Time Management

In the previous chapters we have discussed how to become a better student by using efficient study techniques. Now we are going to discuss how to organize your time so you can use the techniques previously discussed successfully.

Most of us waste enormous amounts of time every day. If you ask yourself what you had for breakfast yesterday, and you are like most people, you probably don't remember. Normally, it is not important to remember what you did or when you did it; however, when you are a student in an intensive program in the sciences or medical education you cannot afford to lose track of or waste time. You need to know not only what you have done, but also what you are going to do and when you are going to do it. This is the only way that work is going to get completed on time without having to do everything at the last minute.

Developing and Maintaining a Schedule

1.   *Determine How You Are Presently Spending Your Time*

The best way to begin to develop a schedule for yourself is to look at how you are already spending your time. Use the form on the next page to keep track of how you spend your time for one week. Write down everything you do while you are doing it. Do not wait till the end of the week and then try to remember what you did. It is important to be specific. If you were studying Chemistry, do not simply put down that you were studying Chemistry; describe what you did. Did you read the textbook, problem-solve, or work on the labs? Include dinner times, travel times, freetime, and sleep time. Give as much detail as possible. The only person who will see this schedule is you, so be honest with yourself.

At the end of the week, examine how you spend your time. Ask yourself where it was used efficiently and where it was wasted. After doing this, develop a new schedule for yourself. The best time to develop this schedule is on Sunday before you begin studying.

2.   *Developing an Effective Schedule*

When you begin to develop your schedule, note your assignments for the week in each of your classes. Estimate how long each of these assignments will take you to complete; then allocate that time on the schedule. Always overestimate the time the task will require. If you think it will take you two hours to complete, put down three. If it takes you only two hours to finish, you have an extra hour you had not counted on; on the other hand, if it takes longer to complete the assignments than you anticipated, there will be time in your schedule to allow for that, and you will not have to find an additional hour, which will usually come from your free time.

When making a schedule, be specific. If you intend to read your Biology textbook, indicate the chapters you plan to complete. Do not simply put down that you are going to study biology, as you will later waste valuable time trying to figure out exactly what you are going to do.

Try to load your heaviest days toward the beginning of the week. This has two advantages: 1) you will tend to be more energetic in the beginning of the week than you are at the end; 2) it will help you complete your reading assignments early in the week; keeping you better prepared for lecture and better able to take good notes in class. Try not to schedule any studying activity for more than two straight hours. It is important to vary studying activities to reduce boredom and fatigue. If you are going to read Biochemistry, read it for two hours, then study some other subject, and then go back to Biochemistry.

3.   *Maintaining a Study Schedule*

Revise your schedule each week. If you do not revise your schedule every week, you will quickly find that your schedule no longer reflects your needs, and you will not follow it. Remember that your demands change each week. Some weeks, you have major exams and need more study time. Other weeks, you may come to a particularly difficult unit and have to increase your study time in that subject, or some week you may have a social engagement which you know will interfere with your usual study time.

Make your time schedule realistic. Do not schedule time the way you think it ought to be, but the way you can realistically study. Don't schedule study time from midnight to three in the morning when you know you can't stay up past eleven o'clock.

Always try to schedule yourself some free time, preferably a free day or evening. It is a good idea to schedule this time towards the end of the week. Give it to yourself as a reward for successfully sticking to the schedule and completing the week's work.

Once you make your weekly schedule, you must have the discipline to stick to it. No schedule will work if you do not follow it. The moment you deviate from your schedule, you will be forced to use your free time to make up for the time you have lost. The result of this is that you will no longer have free time to look forward to at the end of the week and will be less likely to follow the schedule.

Always make two copies of your schedule. Post one in your study area, and take the other one to classes. This will make you constantly aware of what you are supposed to be doing and when you are supposed to be doing it.

There are several advantages to time management. One obvious advantage is that you will be able to complete your assignments on time and not always be catching up. A second major advantage, although a less obvious one, is that you will now know what it takes for you to do well in a class.

Suppose you get an A on a Physics exam. Without an accurate record of what you did to get the A, you have no idea how you got it and may fail to get an A on the next exam. On the other hand, had you been making a time schedule every week, you would know exactly what it took for you to earn that A. Suppose you were not successful on your Physics exam. Without having a time schedule, it is very hard to make the appropriate correction in your study technique so you can improve your grade. If you have been making a study schedule each week, you not only know the amount of time you spent studying Physics, but how you spent it. When you add more time into your schedule for studying physics, you will know what kind of time to add. You can look back and see whether you needed more problem solving time, more time working on the textbook, or more time reviewing lecture notes.

Another advantage to making a time schedule every week and following it is that it will allow you free time that is really free. When you go out on a date on Friday night, you will really be able to enjoy it, because you will know you have completed all your studying and that this free time is really yours. Time management also means that instead of having to use vacation time for catching up, you will be caught up, and vacation time can actually be used to relax and enjoy vacation.

Time management allows for the successful completion of tasks, as well as a certain amount of free time; however, time management only works if you follow your schedule precisely. The moment you fail to follow your schedule, the benefits of time management disappear. This means you must have the discipline not to talk on the telephone when you are supposed to be studying Physiology or go out with a friend when you are supposed to be studying Anatomy. It also means that the schedule must be realistic and include things like travel time, time for meals, and time for friends. Remember that a time schedule only works if you follow it.

Time	Sunday	Monday	Tuesday	Wednesday	Thursday	Friday	Saturday
6 - 7							
7 - 8							
8 - 9							
9 - 10							
10 - 11							
11 - 12							
12 - 1							
1 - 2							
2 - 3							
3 - 4							
4 - 5							
5 - 6							
6 - 7							
7 - 8							
8 - 9							
9 - 10							
10 - 11							
11 - 12							
12 - 1							
1 - 2							
2 - 3							